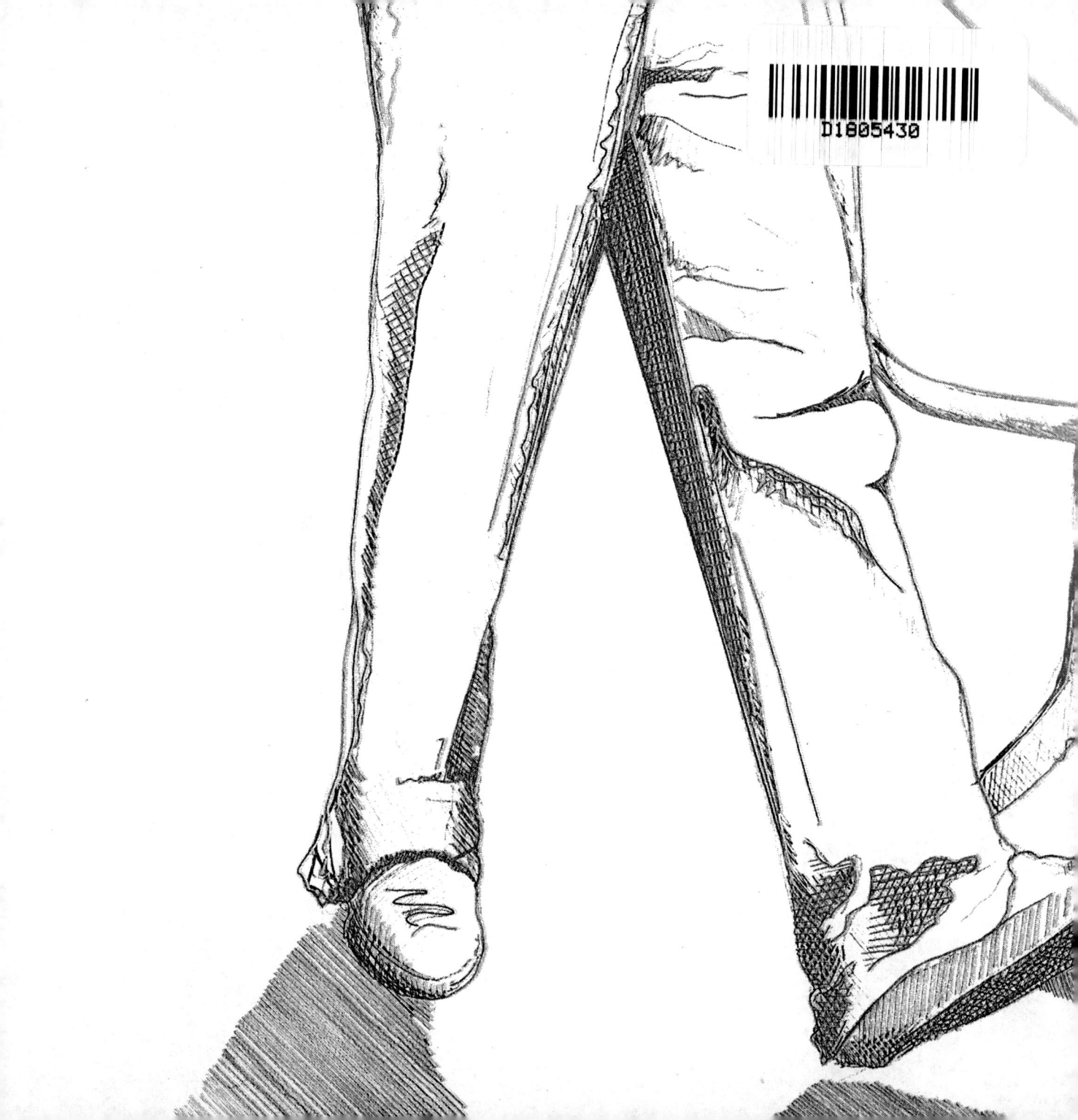

© Robert E. Dahl and Rachel Dahl, 2014.

Unauthorized use and/or duplication of this material without express and written permission from this authors and/or owners are strictly prohibited. Excerpts and links may be used, provided that full and clear credit is given to Robert E. Dahl and Rachel Dahl with appropriate and specific direction to the original content.

What You Have Before You Is A Labor Of Love

I see the dune ahead
and steel for the
climb knowing
that the prize of the
azure waters of Lake
Michigan
lap along the beach just
on the other
side.

The Ten P.M. Walk

Musings, Vignettes, Poems
by Robert E. Dahl

Illustrated Interpretations
& Book Design
by Rachel Dahl

My blog bobdahl.wordpress.com began in September 2011 when readers suggested I move my work from e-mail. Then I expanded stories and essays to include poetry, which is an old love of mine. THEN THE POETRY TOOK OVER. For many years I had followed traditional submission of short stories, articles, essays, and editorials to various publications with 23 professional pieces published. I had already decided to follow a different publishing path but received confirmation of that decision when I read a book on why writers write. Twenty famous writers were interviewed and at the end of each chapter, the writers gave some of their "wisdom" to the reader. Several of the writers suggested, in light of the revolution of publishing, that people publish their own books. And so, I asked several friends and relatives with an interest in my blog to name their ten favorite poems and other musings of mine; in essence, they became my editors, though I have added some of my own choices. You will see their names in the acknowledgments and with their chosen pieces. I asked daughter Rachel if she would illustrate several of the pieces; enthusiastically she agreed and also volunteered to do the complete manuscript layout. What you have before you is a labor of love — my love of poetry, my friends' time of reading and evaluating 370 postings and my daughter's artistic talent and professional expertise. My hope is that you enjoy the result as much as I enjoyed the process.

ACKNOWLEDGMENTS:
Volunteer Editors

Andrea Alter, Jim Berbiglia, Marcia Dahl, Matthew Dahl, Rachel Anna Dahl, Tom Eggebeen, Mary Faust, Marilyn Fox, Sandy Gumm, Vicki VanEck Hill, Lon Liebelt, Chuck Smith, Nick Temple, Martha York.

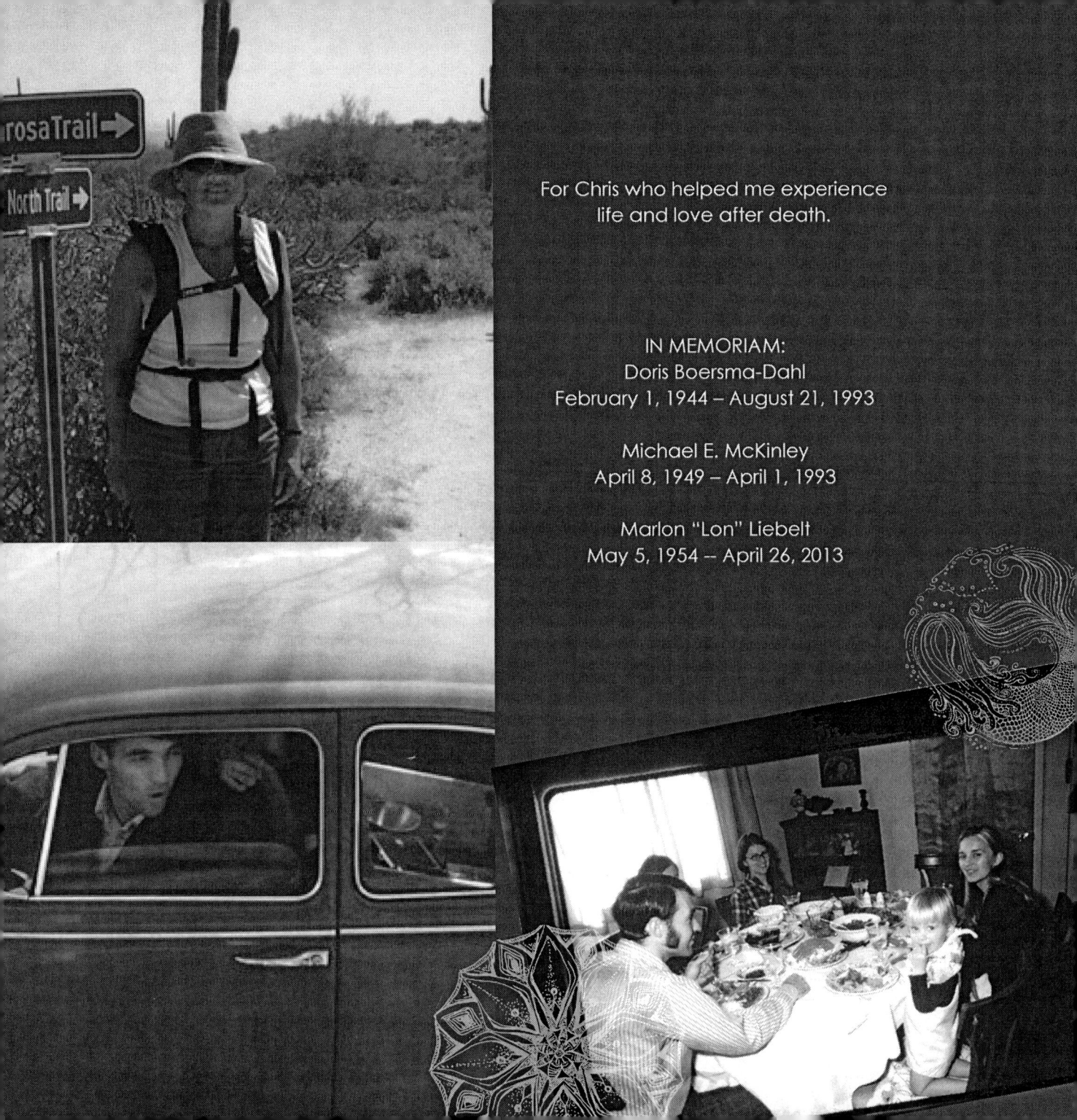

For Chris who helped me experience life and love after death.

IN MEMORIAM:
Doris Boersma-Dahl
February 1, 1944 – August 21, 1993

Michael E. McKinley
April 8, 1949 – April 1, 1993

Marlon "Lon" Liebelt
May 5, 1954 – April 26, 2013

If You Wish to Find Love	15
I Met A Big, Burly Fellow	16
We Live Along the Shore	17
I Went to Visit Dr. Redy	18
Writing Is Dangerous Work	21
We Met the Viper	22
Does the Sterling Silver Cross Burn?	23
Sometimes You Read A Book	24
Man-in-the-Moon Marigolds	25
Watching a Spider and Running a Race	27
As Some Books Electrify	28
The Ten PM Walk	30
The Benefits of Wheat Free Living	32
The Zen Student Asked	35
Leaving	37
She Stares at Her Daughter	39
When Doris Day Sang	41
When He Awoke	43
His Arm	44
The Girl Behind the Fast Food Visor	46
He Simply Said, I'm Sorry	48
The Help Asked	49
Seven Haikus for Boomer	51
Like A Lakota Chief	52
He Resisted the Fame	54
He is a Native American Alcoholic	56
Or Maybe It's Just What I Would Want	57
I'm Just A Poor Old Country Preacher	58
Tears Tumbled	61
The Wind Blew in the Valley	62
Socrates Asked Another Question	63
It Was a Letter from Home	64
Goats Do Roam	66
The SUV Danced and Pranced	68
Quiet, Peaceful	69
The Young Attractive, Black, Female, Law Student	71
On a Sidewalk Sale Saturday	72
Tell Me About Your Life, Dad	73
The Blue Light in the Big Bay Window	74
Throwing Stones – A Short Story	76
Ghazal #2	78
He Entered the Sacred Ground	79
Fire Consumes Wood	80
A Quarter Mile Down the Gravel Road	82
The Proverb Admonishes	85
In the Warmth of Winter	87
He Exited This Life	89
He Impatiently Awaited His Leash	91
Sometimes He Would Call	92
The Big Bay Window	93
He Wondered Where and When	96
Black Friday from the Edge of the Sea	99
Carpentry and Gardening	100
Some People Are Beaten Down So Hard	101
Ecological Racism and Karma	102
Some NSA Guy	103
The Cowboy from Tucson	105
The Religious Rich	106
The String of Jalapeno Lights	108
Way Out in the Wild and Wooly West	109
When Was the Last Time	110

If You Wish to Find Love
(Chosen by Matthew)

If you wish to find love, a true love, just listen
To the voice, one that comes suddenly then hasten
To the heart, to the place, trusted least, but most true,
The one place, a small space, where one finds, riches through
And through — the center, of the heart, to the nerves.
If you just, give me pause, I have limited reserves.
An old man, I have limitations, boundaries,
But you see, I'm still aiming — to please.

I have limitations, boundaries, But you see, I'm still aiming to please.

I Met A Big, Burly Fellow

I met a big, burly fellow the other
day as he emerged
from the pool.
He was in town for a big party.
He's from a rural community in Texas
but he used to live in Tucson and started out in
Phoenix, a senior citizen's lifetime ago.
After a few introductory remarks,
he launched into a diatribe against the dysfunctional
government
and how all things in general are
crappy and how all the empty milk jugs are littering
the South Texas/South Arizona landscape
marring the beauty of the land. I wondered, as he
emerged from the refreshing waters of the pool,
if he thought about the beauty of the water
that had been in those jugs to keep people who
crossed the border in the searing heat alive.
The jugs will be picked up; some will be recycled –
perhaps some made into art in a grade school project.
The landscape remains beautiful with or without
the jugs. People survive. From the hot tub, as the
water swirled around me and as the water dripped
from the suit encompassing his ample girth, I
wished the fellow well.

We Live Along the Shore

We live along the
shore of an
inland sea.
We live in a house
surrounded by grass
of that sea.
We have trees and
plants, birds, bugs
and bees.
What we don't have
are machines that
belch in the breeze.
But, we who live
along the shore
of the sea,
find that tools of
suburbia make
us wheeze.
I'd like our neighbors
to desist and
cease
from use of polluting
machines that make
us sneeze.
But it's too late;
so it wouldn't work
even to say please.
I use my inhaler and
continue to wheeze.
Welcome to the inland
sea with a less than
pure breeze.

I Went to Visit Dr. Redy

(Chosen by Vicki)

I went to visit Dr. Redy
today because my annual
visit was just ready.
I entered the office late
but they weren't ready
for me to see Dr. Redy.
So I sat and watched a
waiting room that was
completely empty.
The staff worked away
on computers to handle
the patients when ready,
but no one seemed this day
to be ready, so I sat and
tried to stay steady,
to keep my blood pressure
low and my breathing really
calm and very steady,
to be really, really ready
to be examined thoroughly
by Dr. Redy.
Finally a nurse in full
pregnant bloom asked
if I were ready.
I said no I was the patient
and not to be confused
with the esteemed Dr. Redy.
Not amused, she stood her ground
and said, "Stand down and remain
very steady."
I asked if she were Redy and she said
she was but she didn't look

much like Dr. Redy,
except she looked ready to drop
the baby but hopefully
not on its heady.
She said for that she had two
more months but that she
was really ready.
Finally, the Dr. named Redy
really was ready. I asked him
if he were really ready
or if I should wait for someone
named Fast Eddie Redy. He said
his name was Freddie not Eddie.
Then steady Freddie Redy moved through
the exam with form ready
and steady.
I told him I had been hoping
for Fast Eddie but was glad
to have now-ready steady
Freddie Redy.
I asked him if he had children
and he looked at me and
said, "Nadayettee."
I said, "Well, Doc, you
ain't get'n younger so you
better getta ready.
He said he had a girl
who was Nadayettee.
"Not a yettee what?" I asked
Dr. Freddie Redy.
"Nadayettee
Redy."

So I sat and
tried to stay steady,
to keep my blood pressure
low and my breathing really
calm and very steady
to be really, really ready

"Not a yettee ready for what?"
"Nadayettee Redy is who she is."
"What isn't she ready for?"
"Well, she's only thirteen,
my Nadayettee Redy."
Who's on first and What's
on second? I sure wasn't steady.
I thought of Abbott and Costello,
and Laurel and Hardy.
Oh, I was feeling really
not ready for
steady Dr. Freddie Redy.
He told me I passed
the physical and to stop
being so very petty
and to turn on my heels and
quick step to the desk
of the secretary,
who, to take my money
for the exam, was
surely ready.
I told him I once dated
a really cute girl
named Shirley Redy
and that she surely was
ready unlike his little
Nadayettee.
He just collapsed in
the chair to stay steady.
I gave him a wave and said,
"See you next year, Steady
Freddie,
and when I arrive, I hope
you really will be really fast
and ready, steady Dr. Freddie
Redy."

Writing Is Dangerous Work

Writing is dangerous work writes
the novelist, toxic even.
Toxins rise to the surface of the
psyche while the writer
sits at the writing desk, pen to
paper. It is hazardous duty –
this novel writing he writes, but
alluring he seemingly
concedes – tantalizing and tasty
to flirt with the dirt
deep in one's own soul. A bit of
a poet, he writes that the
tastiest place of the fugu fish is
nearest the poison.
Novelists sit close to the poison.
Sometimes novelists
fondle the fish dish too long, inhale too
deeply and taste the poisonous
flesh of the fish. This novelist is a
marathon runner who
sweats out the toxins after sitting at
his desk flirting with those
poisons for hours at a time. Do poets
know the danger and cozy
up only in spurts to the poisons and
then sprint away to cozy
up another day like a track athlete
running a hundred,
two hundred or four hundred
meters at a time at
most?

We Met the Viper
(Chosen by Vicki, Marcia)

We met the viper along the trail but never did we think we would meet him again on the landing of our condo. He sweet-talked his way into our home and spun a tale; the rattling behind him should have been a give away, but, on face value, he was such a charming snake with such a pretty tail. We gave him the keys to our kingdom, left for the summer and waited and waited to hear from him about his end of the bargain, but that end just rattled and rattled. How do you shake hands with a snake? I felt the firm grip, but now I rub my fingers together and feel only slippery skin. The snake in the grass sleeps in our bed with quiet tail curled around the post. Now, it's in the hands of the sheriff to uncoil the tail of the teller of tales while we, Adam and Eve, look back from somewhere east of Eden.

Does the Sterling Silver Cross Burn?
(Chosen by Rachel)

A big, butterfly tattoo on her left shoulder-blade,
a cute curly cue on her right buttocks,
a bare bones something or other engraved on her left triceps,

and surrounded by a spider web tattoo, a
sterling silver cross piercing her belly button,

she coos sweetly and lovingly lowers her little boy
into the hot tub with her while the cross dangles.

They sit and she asks questions in two-year-old talk.
Does the cross burn her tummy?

The little boy plays on deck while mommy
bathes in the sun.

Does the cross burn a mark on her tummy?
Does the mark then heal, peel and fade?

Sometimes You Read A Book
(Chosen by Vicki)

Sometimes you read
a book that leaves
you — face flushing,
heart pounding,
pulse surging,
throat tightening,
eyes tearing,
scared as a
Jack Rabbit hopping
into the path
of a coiled
Western Rattler
lurking under the
dead branch of
a Cholla just waiting
to strike and the last
few pages struck
hard and fast and
the venom rushes
through literary veins
causing the paralysis
of addiction, the rare
antidote known as
the highly touted
sequel.

Man-in-the-Moon Marigolds

In the middle of the summer he froze in the pulpit just as he was expounding on the play "The Effect of Gamma Rays on Man-in-the-Moon Marigolds" and its relation to the lectionary Gospel reading for the day in common time. It was anything but common for him or for the congregation. Concerned elders escorted the catatonic preacher from the pulpit to the hospital. He was a man consumed with preaching the Realm of God with all its social justice implications. He was a prophet, but he was also a priest who ached for his people and held their hands and shed tears with them over the years. Many in the pews had looked daggers at him for his courage and one day after many, many Sundays of seeing those faces from the pulpit, he felt zapped like a marigold and just froze. Months later he re-entered the pulpit and finished the meaning of the illustration of "The Effect of Gamma Rays on Man-in-the-Moon Marigolds" in relation to the lectionary Gospel reading of a few months before. He veered off the lectionary course, but he had something to finish for that particular day about the value and endurance of Man-in-the-Moon Marigolds. In Mexico marigolds are the flower of choice for El Dia De Los Muertos because they bloom in November. In this particular November, it was for a resurrection not a celebration of the dead. When he said amen and sat down, the choir stood and sang before the offering was taken, as usual.

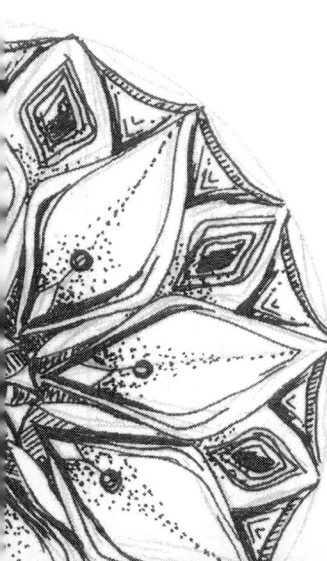

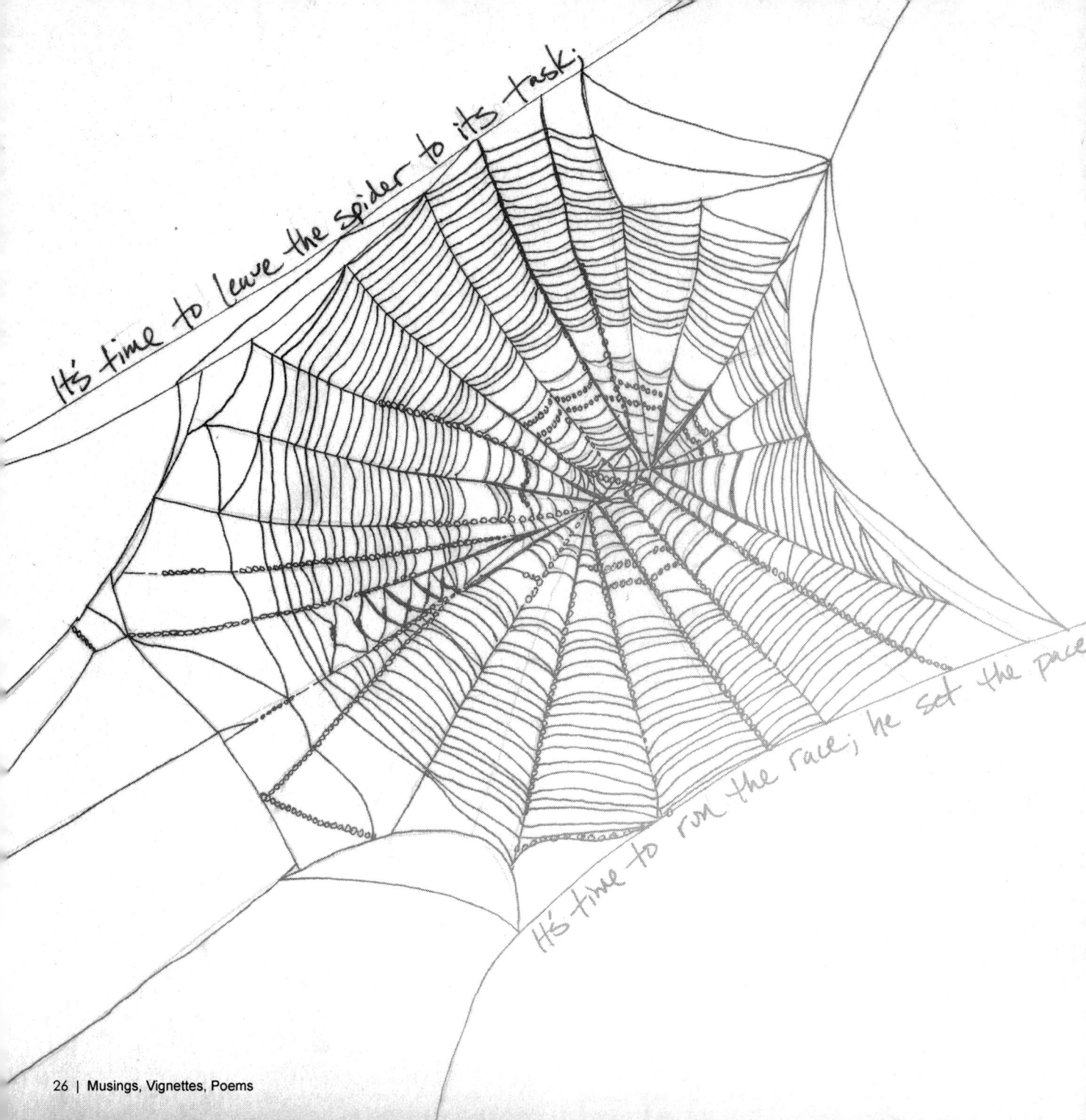

Watching a Spider and Running a Race
(Chosen by Rachel, Nick, Vicki)

She watched the spider spin her winter's web;
A runner ran against the wind that day.
The arachnoid swung back and forth in bed;
The woman watched the runner making hay.

It's time to leave the spider to its task;
It's time to run the race; he set the pace.
She flexed her toes and knew she could run fast,
And smiled as she blew by to end the race.

As Some Books Electrify

(Chosen by Vicki)

As some books
electrify to the marrow
of the bones,
others, recommended
strongly by timid
souls hiding for
months if not years
in their hideaway
habitats while
proclaiming
ego release and
spiritual awakening
and inner strength,
leave the flesh flaccid
– every last paragraph
of every chapter (a
suggestion for scanning
by a former English
prof.) from first to
last was just all the
same
boring
stuff
with all the banal
self-help sentiments and
jargon wrapped in
superficial Judeo/Christ-
ian, Hindu, Buddhist
and, of course, humanist

pseudo-something
thrown in to appeal
to those slipping
away from forty-three
years of traditional
interpretation of the
doctrines to
enlightened table-talk
with the supposedly
well-educated, academ-
ically credentialed
professionals hiding
in their own hideaway
habitats out of which
they venture on
occasion, particularly
if there is an
audience or, perhaps
even more fashionably, a
soiree of retirees.

The Ten PM Walk
(Chosen by Jim, Mary, Tom, Chris)

On Tuesday, they had to euthanize their
twelve-year-old Chocolate Lab.

On Tuesday, Wednesday and Thursday
at ten p.m. and perhaps for every evening
in the foreseeable future for

however long it would take, the man picked
up his mesquite hiking stick and his 225
lumen, compact flashlight

and headed down the stairs of the condo
to walk his dog. He made his way
through the back parking

lot with a lighted hill on his left leading to the
upper swimming pool and condos on his right.
He watched the blue, flickering light

in some and wondered if any of the darkened
condos were in foreclosure. He listened
to the sounds of the fountain

as he passed. The cascading water reminded
him, in a small way, of home and the waves
of Lake Michigan where his dog

had loved to romp. Periodically, he would
depress the button of the flashlight
half-way to spot flash along

the hill. Once he spooked a coyote at rest.
At the end of the parking lot, the trail
began which led to an underpass

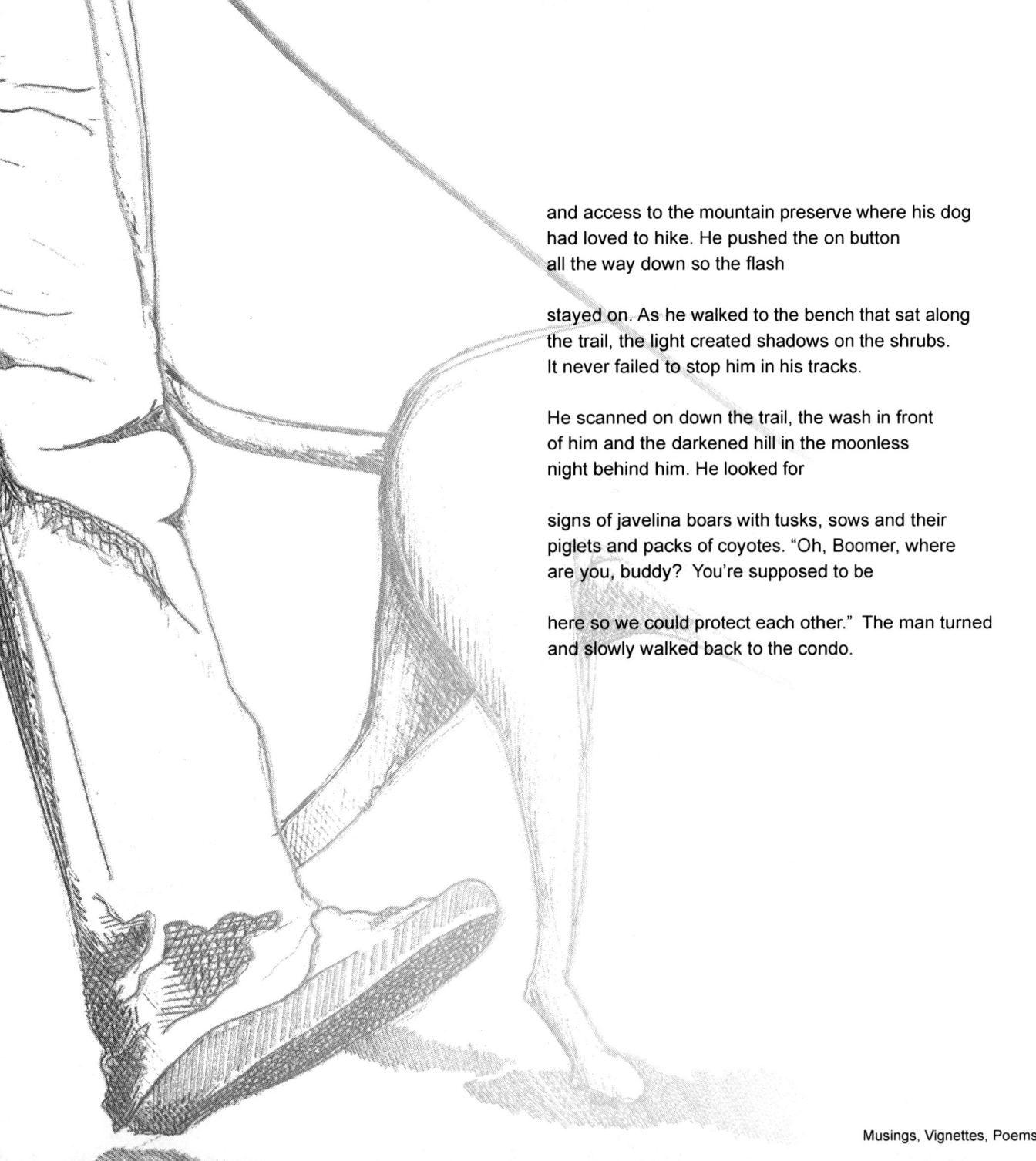

and access to the mountain preserve where his dog
had loved to hike. He pushed the on button
all the way down so the flash

stayed on. As he walked to the bench that sat along
the trail, the light created shadows on the shrubs.
It never failed to stop him in his tracks.

He scanned on down the trail, the wash in front
of him and the darkened hill in the moonless
night behind him. He looked for

signs of javelina boars with tusks, sows and their
piglets and packs of coyotes. "Oh, Boomer, where
are you, buddy? You're supposed to be

here so we could protect each other." The man turned
and slowly walked back to the condo.

The Benefits of Wheat Free Living

(Article chosen by Jim, Mary, Tom)

A week ago I e-mailed many friends about the touted benefits of refraining from eating wheat. The claim is that wheat plants are treated with toxins by agribusiness to grow fuller crops which can get to market faster. Apparently, the toxins don't go away in the processing from plant to flour and have negative effects on our health.

An acquaintance raved about the benefits for his and his wife's arthritis. After three days wheat free, they were pain-free. I looked up an article on the internet and read that people who quit wheat watched pounds melt right off their bodies, saw their good cholesterol skyrocket and their blood pressure drop through the floor. I couldn't wait to get started.

Here is the update I promised those friends. I didn't think it would come this quickly but I have hard and fast evidence of the results of giving up wheat and its benefits for the body, not to mention mind and spirit.

My wife and I wondered what we would do to find substitutes for wheat. The young woman in the condo immediately beneath us, a veteran of five years wheat free, helped immeasurably. We had already purchased a package of organic brown rice pasta, but she gave us another brand that she thought was better and actually gave us the gift of a package. She said we could do a taste test.

Also, instead of wheat crackers for our cheese snacks, we found rice crackers and low-calorie rice cakes.

Knowing that most vodka was made from wheat, I visited the local grocery store and discovered a potato vodka for a fairly reasonable price. At an upscale liquor store, the clerk introduced me to some upscale vodka made from grapes. Grapes, of course. I didn't buy the vodka but I did buy lots of Pinot Grigio. Red wine gives me a headache. No wheat in wine.

And so the experiment began.

We had brown rice pasta each night with various wheat free sauces and meats with a small side salad, of course. The left overs became breakfast with a different sauce under melted cheese (no wheat in cheese) and topped with two poached eggs (the healthiest way to prepare an egg). The neighbor's pasta choice was a bit better we decided. When the pasta ran out we turned to rice, brown rice, lots and lots of brown rice for dinner with delicious sauces. We looked forward to trying the brown rice with wild rice. When the rice ran out, we used baked potatoes as our veggie with delicious rib-eye steak grilled medium rare. Can't get enough great protein from grass-fed beef. No wheat there. Each meal was washed down with the reasonably priced wine.

For another meal we bought brown rice hamburger buns. They were delicious buttered and toasted on the grill to be used with the luscious hamburgers I grilled and topped with delicious, melted Irish cheddar cheese with shallots. The left overs again were used for breakfast. The brown rice hamburger buns became buttered (no butter substitute) toast served with organic jelly and organic peanut butter. The left-over burger was used in a three-cheese, three-egg omelette (poached is so mundane after a while).

Being full from breakfast, we didn't need another meal till dinner so for a snack those brown rice crackers and rice cakes came in handy with the cheese (one can't get enough organic cheese), sardines and smoked oysters in oil for happy hour to go with our potato vodka. If we wanted to go out for happy hour we found a great deal at a local Mexican restaurant: two corn tortilla (no wheat flour for us) tacos with ground beef, rice and refried beans which we split, of course, for $4.95 and $1 Margaritas. Those babies do go down like soda pop.

After dinner, wanting something a little sweet but healthy and wheat free to finish off the day, we bought some absolutely delicious, organic dark chocolate peanut butter cups and one (or several), wee little night-cap to go along.

So here are the amazing results after just one week. Oh, as an aside, I decided to clean up my appearance to go with my new resolution to eat healthy in the new year so I shaved my head.

Well, back to the results. I have gained seven pounds in seven days and before going to bed, after all that wheat free wine and vodka, I look like a giant, round, white, bobble head bowling ball. I have found that in the morning, the bobbling continues but with significant pain for a while. By happy hour the pain is usually gone and afterward, it is definitely gone.

One morning, wife Chris informed me that on the previous evening I single-handedly had attempted to re-enact the entire Bolshoi Ballet much to the distress of the young woman in the condo below. Fortunately, I had no recollection of any such behavior and am inclined to think my wife is pulling my leg. She's such a kidder.

By the end of the evening, I'm having such a good time, I don't really give a damn about the cholesterol or blood pressure, but in the morning I am panicked that my HDL is burrowing its way to China and my LDL is skyrocketing to the moon. I'm glad my cholesterol test is next August. That will give me a chance to turn things around. And I don't dare get anywhere near the blood pressure machine at the local pharmacy for fear that if I took my blood pressure, alarms would go off and the EMT would show up.

But, hey, you can't expect success on all fronts. I have had zero pain in the arthritic middle knuckle on my left-hand pinkie.

Cheers!

Bob

The Zen Student Asked
(Chosen by Nick, Marcia, Marilyn)

The Zen student asked
the master,
"How do you see
so much?"
"I close my eyes."
I sit in my easy chair
with my feet crossed
on the ottoman.
I close my eyes and
see and smell red,
white and jack pines.
I watch the trail for
hazardous, ancient roots
hidden under shiny,
slippery oak leaves.
I feel the cushion made
by seasons of pine
needles as I jog at a
slow, steady, comfortable
pace.
I see the dune ahead
and steel for the
climb knowing
that the prize of the
azure waters of Lake Michigan
lap along the beach just
on the other
side.

I pick up the pace just a
bit and stare at the shoe
impressions made by
others in the damp,
firm sand.
I stop before returning
to the woods, rest
my hands on my knees,
catch my breath while
thinking about
the climb
back up soft sand
that gives way
under each step.
I look around.
For the moment
I am alone with
the forest, dunes,
beach, and inland
sea.
I can't see across,
but I feel like
I can see
everything.

Leaving
(Chosen by Martha, Sandy)

Leaving the
reunion
a man was
approached
by a classmate
with whom
he reconnected
after about forty-
eight years. They
had shared over
a drink in the bar
away from the
other classmates.
The classmate
embraced the
man, held him
tightly and when
it seemed
appropriate
to the man to let
go, the classmate
whispered in his
ear, "Don't let
go yet. Please."
In that moment,
all the

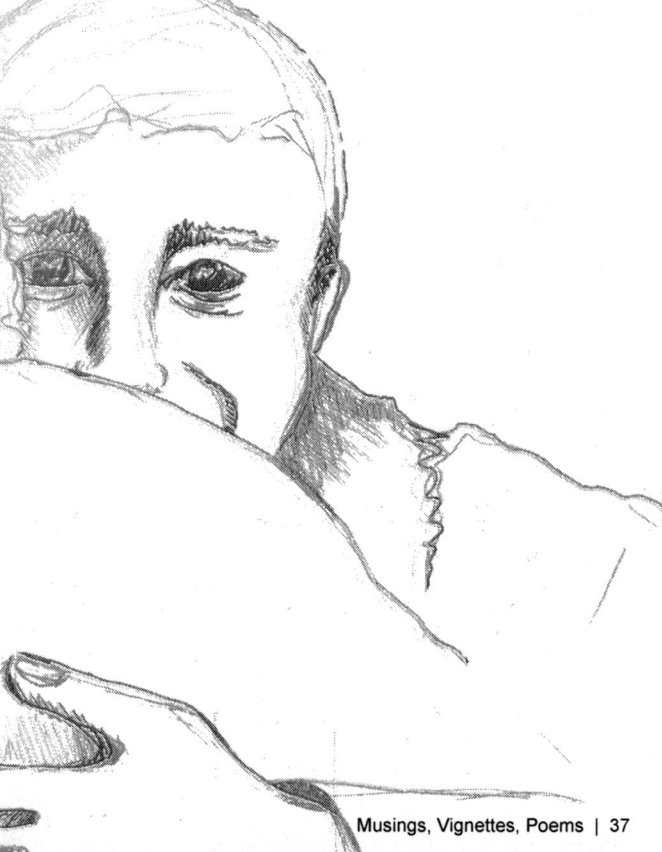

stupid,
rude,
dumb-assed
noise
around
them faded in-
to the distance.
Two needy
guys held
each other
up like a
piling in
a storm
holding
the pier
in place.

She Stares at Her Daughter
(Chosen by Martha, Andrea)

His thirty-nine-year-old daughter called to tell him
that her twenty-two-month-old daughter is beginning

to look like his daughter's mother who died when his
daughter was twenty. She tells him she just sits and

stares at her daughter seeing who was in who is and
probably wondering what is to be. She hasn't seen,

touched or kissed her mother in nineteen years, half her
life ago, but she can see, touch and kiss her all over

again, differently, now as the mother, in the baby's blue
eyes and blond hair and the baby face before her, in the

one who came out of her own womb just as she had come
out of her mother's. He tells her to keep staring because

before she knows it, her daughter will be up and out. He doesn't
know if she liked that idea very much. She probably doesn't

want to contemplate another loss of a loved one even if it
means years still down the line, just out of the house and down

the block or maybe even another state or country. She lifts
and holds her daughter lightly and gently like an unopened

package marked fragile which just arrived in the mail, holds
the image before her eyes, gently inhales and smells the hair

just like her mother's, kisses the damp top of her daughter's
head just like her mother used to kiss the top of her head. Even

though she wants to, she doesn't hold her daughter too tightly
out of some abandonment fear because the child would

just wiggle free like a baby brookie in a fast mountain stream and skip
out early. She knows it happens a lot. She cradles her daughter

and begins to hum "Rock a Bye Baby" just like her mother hummed
to her thirty some years ago. A tear falls on her daughter's cheek.

His daughter leans over and kisses the tear savoring the saltiness.

When Doris Day Sang
(Chosen by Martha, Lon, Chris)

When Doris Day sang through
the night club smoke as it wafted
over her passing through her
flowing golden locks and chiffon
gown, but apparently not affecting
her voice, "The magic is my love for
you," and it was the summer of
1953 and I'm eight years old and
standing in my underpants as the
wind blows through the open wind-
ows of the second floor of our
south side of Chicago home and my
mother, over the sound of the radio,
shouts up the stairwell, "Robert Edwin,
you better not be bouncing on your bed."
Jeannie Hedstrom and I broke that up-
stairs make-do trampoline the week
before. I shout back, "I'm just standin'
here, mom," as I slip into the bathroom
and Doris Day gives way to Kate
Smith's "God Bless America."

He Stood Over the Kitchen Sink

(Chosen by Martha, Lon)

As when a single drop
of white vinegar

first touches
baking soda,

his tears erupted
spontaneously

when the first
word about his now
dead dog

emerged from his
lips and touched

the dry, desert air.

And then one day
as another word

emerged, he thought
about the tear

as it, too, emerged
but just a moment
later,

and knew, it was time
to let the air dry

the tear and cry

no more

when he spoke
of his

now dead dog.

When He Awoke
(Chosen by Lon, Mary)

When he awoke, he
Wondered
Why
He had dreamed
What he had dreamed
At the beginning of March –
No birthdays, no anniversaries,
And then he thought
About the death of his dog
Three weeks before.
Would it? Could it?
The death of a pet
Triggering a
Dream
About his wife of twenty-six
Years
Who died almost twenty years
Before?
This time
He told his wife,
Who, for the first time, instead
Of turning from him,
Wanted him to stay with
Her at her art exhibit,
That he had to go.
She had always left
Him
In his sweat as he
Had emerged
So very, very
Sad from sleep.
He wondered aloud,
"Had the dog
Meant that
Much?"

His Arm
(Chosen by Lon, Tom, Marilyn)

There was something in him
that was out of control – his
arm. He had been on his way –
Little League All Star, Kiwanis
All Star. His dad had worked
with him, hour after hour, on
his hitting, fielding and throwing
and then his dad just up and died.
Then in high school, he still hit
and fielded skillfully, but he could
no longer throw the ball straight
from left field, center field or
right. They put him on first base
where they thought he would
do the least damage and when
he couldn't throw the ball from
first to home anymore, the coach,
back in the day, said the politically
incorrect thing: "Just roll it in,
girly." For the next several years
he kept his life together, more
or less, and then he saw Steve
Sax, second baseman for the
Los Angeles Dodgers and
premier professional baseball
player, lose his throwing arm
and Steve couldn't throw the
ball from second to first and
he wondered what Steve
was going through and he
thought that if it could happen
to such a great player as Steve,

it could happen to him, for
whatever reason and he took
comfort in Steve's misery and
he figured out that his arm went
crazy after his dad died and that
his arm was still out in left field
and would ever and always be
there and while he felt really bad
for Steve Sax, he gave thanks for
his wild left arm, the arm
coaches thought would be his ticket
to the big leagues, the arm that
went crazy after his dad died
– the arm that took and absorbed
all the grief and let him find his
way out of left field and
into life.

The Girl Behind the Fast Food Visor

(Chosen by Mary, Andrea, Sandy)

Having stared at the dollar menu he had memorized but does because it just seems part of the routine, he approached (having known before he entered the door exactly what he was going to order) the counter and heard

exactly what he knew he was going to hear before he said what he was going to order. "Welcome. May I take your order?" He hardly heard her and momentarily forgot what it was he was going to order,

which he had known forever because it was what he always orders. She was short and had her visor pushed forward and down covering her eyes. She looked up just long enough to greet him and it was

then he saw her eye and the left side of her face. He quickly looked at her name-tag and she just as quickly looked back down at the register. A patch of grayish, plastic like skin had been attached tautly to the side of her face on top

of the cheekbone and the skin around her eye was scar tissue and red mucous membrane rimmed the eyeball and he wondered how she blinked. Congenital, a fire, a drunken father's blow with a fireplace poker, a car crash?

He wondered if the kids at school ever taunted her or if she would be asked to the prom. He wondered if she ever looked anyone straight in the eye. The nanosecond was an eternity of wondering. He thought of the Buddha and that all of life was suffering, and he didn't want her to suffer anymore. He wanted to shout silently "Heal!" and he wanted fresh, new pink skin to form on her cheekbone and an eyelid and long beautiful lashes to grow under the Fast Food

visor and he wanted her to push that visor up and back and wink a coquettish wink at him with her left eye. "May I have a Sausage Muffin, please?" "For here or to go?" "For here, Leah. What a beautiful name for a beautiful young lady."

She continued to stare straight ahead at the register with her visor pulled forward and down and said, "Thank you very much." He could see her lips and he thought/hoped he could see a little smile but she never looked him in the eye.

He moved down the counter to wait in the waiting place for the Sausage Muffin, opened the wrapper, lifted the bun, squirted some ketchup on the sausage, replaced the bun, closed the wrapper, grabbed two napkins, sat down by the window

as he always does in the routine, turned to look out of the window opposite the counter like maybe a passing car caught his attention, or like he was watching a little girl slide down the slide into her father's arms

and then he started to cry.

He Simply Said, I'm Sorry
(Chosen by Mary, Marcia, Marilyn)

Three months ago, the man said
goodbye to his twelve-year-old
Chocolate Lab who died in
the man's wife's arms.

A week ago, the man said
goodbye to the congregation
he could no longer attend
in good conscience.

Two days from now the man
will travel to Chicago to say
goodbye in a eulogy to a
friend who committed suicide

on the thirtieth anniversary of
his friend's father's suicide.
This day the man sat in a
deli dining area of a local

grocery store eating a fresh
salad he put together at the
salad bar when a friend who
he hadn't seen in five months

because they winter in different
places sat down. The man just
started to cry and his friend not
knowing anything, except about

the dog's death, but not about the
man's own father's suicide so many,
many years ago, simply said,
"I'm sorry."

The Help Asked
(Chosen by Jim, Marilyn)

The help asked for help for tuition for
her honor roll twins to go to college – a black
school up in some backwater, southern town.

So she built up the courage to ask massa and
missa just at the end of breakfast while they
were finishing up reading the morning

paper, him the sports, her the editorial. Massa
heard the word loan, jumped to his feet, kissed
his blond haired wife goodbye and left.

Missa condescendingly listened and told the
help that she needed to show her independence –
independence she actually said – by earning

the money, being self-sufficient and finding
dignity in self-determination. She said all that
to the help who quietly slipped back into

the kitchen. Years but only a motion picture day
later, a candidate for president of the United States
of America, a child of privilege from a

northern state, said virtually the same thing,
as strategy to kick-start the economy, to those
who needed a low-interest loan with

determination to repay. Learn self-reliance,
and the dignity of self-determination as he,
the self-made man, had. The words were

uttered with the same scorn heard in the
inflection of missa back in the day, but
the words came out muffled and

hardly understandable to those who
heard because of the silver spoon
still in his mouth.

Seven Haikus for Boomer

(Chosen by Nick, Marilyn)

I'm breathing well;
my chocolate lab is not –
my asthma, his throat.

I know how he feels –
inability to breathe
freely and deeply.

Panic lurks close by,
always ready to attack –
shallow breathing, fear.

Our baby Boomer
panting, slurping water,
begging for relief.

Maybe another
doggie prozac will help him
settle down and sleep.

Now I lay me down
to sleep. I pray the Lord
Boomer's life to keep.

If he should die be-
fore I wake, I pray his soul
to heaven does take.

Like A Lakota Chief
(Chosen by Nick, Marilyn)

Cameron sits on the
cement bench on
the side of the
Dreamy Draw Trail
like a Lakota Chief
sits alone meditating
before the council
gathers.
He comes at dark
and smokes
cigarettes
like the chief smokes
a peace pipe to close
the council meeting.
He is a recent
graduate of the
University of Arizona
in mathematics.
He works as an intern
at a computer firm
to expand his field
of expertise before
starting his Ph.D
program at a school
as of yet to be
determined.
He sits through the
cold, clear winter
night and watches the
January full moon.
He sits through the
summer night,
looks up and lets
the monsoon rains
wash over his face.
A lone coyote wanders
past.

He Resisted the Fame

(Chosen by Nick, Lon, Marilyn)

He resisted the fame,
    The notoriety, the
        Money.
A nice guy, bartender,
    Single young
        Man
Put himself at some
    Risk, video
        Taped
The infamous 47%
    Speech which
        May
Have brought down
    The candidacy of
        One
Willard Mitt Romney
    Exposing him
        For
His true, elitist, 50,000
    Dollar a plate
        Beliefs.
The bartender only videoed
    The speech because
        He
Thought he might get
    Invited to have
        Some

Time afterward with
    The candidate and
        All
The other employees
    (Like Billy Clinton
        Did)
But which, of course, never
    Happened because
        It
Would mean that Mitt would
    Be associating with
        Some
Of the 47%. Early one
    Morning when the
        Bartender
Went to take a pee, he looked
    In the mirror and
        Said,
"You are a coward," and
    The rest is history
        Thanks
To a young bartender
    With a
        Conscience.

He is a Native American Alcoholic
(Chosen by Nick, Sandy)

He is a Native American alcoholic,
bi-polar poet, whose stories are his
God and not the Hebrew,
Christian, Muslim nor even the Native
American God or Gods – Mother Earth,
Father Sun, et. al.
He is an angry prophet mad for his
people but mad at his people, too – all of
them who have killed
themselves with booze including most of
the people in his family, clan, tribe, nation.
He reminds me of my late
friend, a German American, alcoholic, bi-
polar genius with an encyclopedic mind
and poetic voice haunted
by the suicide of his father thirty years
before my friend put a gun to his head
and pulled the trigger –
an angry Lakota, an angry German Amer-
ican from North Dakota – a lonely Native
American poetic voice for
justice, a now silent poetic, operatic voice
of exquisite beauty heard only in the hearts of
his conflicted loved ones
– the two separated only by a hair's
breadth or more vividly a hare's
breath on the frozen Dakota
tundra.

Or Maybe It's Just What I Would Want
(Chosen by Sandy, Chris)

A Saudi poet wrote a poem directly to Mohammed
recently and landed in prison. I hope I don't land
in prison, Jesus, but here's one to you.

I don't think you would want me to fall on my face
before you and grasp for the tassels adorning the fringe
of your robe or rub your feet with precious oil from a
broken alabaster jar after brushing the dust from
your well-worn sandals.

I don't think you would want me to attend your
every need as you recline around the dinner table
or hang on your every word spoken around
the camp fire. All that's been done.

I think you would want (or maybe it's what I would
want) me to stand, look straight into your ever so
dark brown Semitic eyes with my blue Scandinavian
eyes, hold out my hand and then embrace you
strongly and tightly and then softly and warmly.

I think I would tell you what I think you would
want to tell me, that I love you.

Then I think about my friend, a connoisseur of
fine food, a sommelier, a basso baritone — Wagner's
Dutchman and Wotan/Der Wanderer, a human
encyclopedia, a generous soul offering gifts of

dark chocolate and real French french roast coffee
and a brandy only a few had ever heard of and a wit
and sometimes a nitwit, a description we all share,
who just killed himself, Jesus, so I can't hug him anymore.

So, I guess you will have to look into his blue Germanic
eyes with your ever so dark brown Semitic eyes, hold out
your hand to him, embrace him strongly and tightly and
softly and warmly and tell him, "I love you," for me.

I'm Just A Poor Old Country Preacher

(Chosen by Sandy, Matthew)

"I'm just a poor, old, country preacher" was the ruse he had learned in the great Commonwealth of Kentucky from his southern born brothers in the ministry.

A city boy from the North, he sat mesmerized by those from Alabama and Mississippi who had journeyed as far north as they could stand and landed in Louisville, south side of the Ohio River,

only venturing beyond the north side of the Ohio for judicatory business, the business of doing the Lord's work having to negotiate about that work with the dreaded Yankees of Civil War infamy.

Years and years before he had ventured south of the Ohio river and almost to the banks of the Cumberland, a man-child in the promised land of Bowling Green, Franklin and Round Pond.

How in the heck did that happen? He asked himself and his wife asked him and his year and a half old son would have asked him if he had thought of it and could formulate the words.

It seemed even to be a question on the lips of the Lord who it has been said wouldn't venture north of Munfordville because anything north of Munfordville was too far north for any self-respecting southern deity.

His daughter, a Southern Belle born way down in Bowling Green where you would find the prettiest girls ever seen, never thought to ask him that because, well, she is a Southern Belle.

He felt like a fish out of water, certainly the great waters of one of the Great Lakes --Lake Michigan, where he would put a toe or two into in July and most certainly early August,

but he got used to putting his hand into the warm waters of the ponds of his farmer parishioners pulling out a catfish or slabber blue gill or really large, largemouth bass.

And he and his son who was now old enough to hold a rod and reel in his hand and make pretty good casts into the ponds and his wife who always brought her art pad to draw and Southern Belle baby

drove through the gates into the fields parking near the pond and the really big fat hogs would come and rub their really dirty bodies against his really nice, white 1970 Dodge Challenger,

and Jack, the owner of the property and an elder in his church, would yell, "Soo-ee, Soo-ee, soo-ee!" and the pigs would prance off to other parts of the pasture.

The transplanted Yankee pastor had been told on the first Sunday that his four and half year tenure began that he had two strikes against him: "One, you're a Yankee. Two, you're from a big city.

And if I might I add three, you're a Presbyterian." "What?" he asked. "This is a Presbyterian Church." "No. That's just the sign above the door. We're really all Baptists here."

He was right. The Yankee preacher's Southern Belle daughter was baptized when she was a month old and when it came to adding up the stats at the end of the year, they just flat out forgot that one

because it hadn't happened by immersion in Drake's Creek.

And so, he went to judicatory meetings to watch with wonder the smooth tongued Presbyterian pastors who sought to outwit each other by using the "I'm just a poor, old Country preacher" ploy,

And it was such a wonder to behold, but there was no greater wonder than the sight of these Southern Presbyterian boys disarming and then sentencing to death by embarrassment their northern counterparts at synod meetings.

Years and years later long after he had ventured back north, he attended a city council meeting to plead the cause of a minority, which wasn't having its rights protected, and he

summoned his best "I'm just a poor, old, country preacher" wily subterfuge, after all he had been an English major with a speech and theater minor in college, with a Kentucky twang and all.

Five minutes after his speech he said, "Thaaank, yu'll very much and praise God!" Then he sat down and three minutes later two of the seven council members smiled.

Tears Tumbled

(Chosen by Matthew, Chris)

Harrison's poems of the north country
and way out west
moved me to fish and hike and reaffirm
the outdoors is best,
and Transtromer his few but Nobel words
slight tomes would wrest
me from my literary loquaciousness and
know that less is best,
but Charlotte's Web brought tears tumbling
to this old man's chest.

The Wind Blew in the Valley
(Chosen by Rachel, Chris)

The wind blew in the valley.
The Javelina sang
with a diaphragmatic belly.
And Piestewa felt a pang

of great regret and grief
that the Diamond-back rattler left
and made off like a thief
with a Gila of great heft.

He crawled back in his hole
but the Gila's head got stuck.
The Trickster came and stole
but the Gila began to buck

and twist and squirm and snap
the coyote's Achilles heel.
So Piestewa laid a trap
while Javelina let out a squeal –

from the valley below
the Spirit rose on high,
tapped the Trickster's elbow
and the dog thought he would die

as he slid down on his belly
while the wind blew in the valley.

Socrates Asked Another Question

(Chosen by Matthew, Chris)

Someone asked
him accusingly
"Do you pray?"
"Yes," he replied.
"Why?" someone
asked. "Because I
don't have all the
answers," he said.
"Would you stop
if you did?" some-
one asked. "If I did
what?" he asked.
"Have all the answers,"
someone said. "Do you
think if I had as
many questions as
Socrates had before
someone handed
him the hemlock,
someone would
hand me the hem-
lock, too?" he asked.
"But what if you had
all the answers?" some-
one asked. "What if I
did?" he asked. "Well,
would you still pray?"
someone asked.
"Would I?" he asked
someone.

It Was a Letter from Home

(Chosen by Lon, Chris)

It was a "Letter from
Home" that made
him so sad.
He stood in the kitchen
and the tears began
to form to
the horn's mournful cry –
a mother to her son in
1944 somewhere in
harm's way?
A critic wrote, wistful.
Copeland's own longing –
that of a single man from
his flat in New York
but spoken in folk tune,
middle America
plain speak?
Longing, a universal chord
is struck – longing,
yearning for that which
is so far away in time
and space but so near
to a breaking heart.
The music crescendos

fortissimo and cascades
to the still, soft, simple
strings of everyone's
heart – longing
in the deep, quiet, achingly
long notes of the clarinet, then
the passing of everyday
chit-chat to mask the
yearning, petitioning,
praying. A young girl's
note to a mother missed
so much?
In an apartment somewhere,
everywhere, a lover pleads
with the Beloved,
"Please come home.
Please."

Goats Do Roam

The article below appeared on the National Geographic's website which was coordinated with the 2009 documentary about our national parks, "The National Parks: America's Best Idea" by Ken Burns . National Geographic asked for accounts of first time visits to a national park:

Goats Do Roam Even Into Weddings at the Grand Canyon

The first time I visited the Grand Canyon was the occasion of the wedding of my daughter Rachel Anna on May 24, 2008. In 1993, Rachel's mother, who was an artist, died of a cerebral hemorrhage at the age of 49. Rachel was 20. The family — I, Rachel and her 25-year-old brother Matthew were devastated. We each began a pilgrimage of grief. Several years later, Rachel decided to spread her wings and venture to Phoenix, Arizona to live with a friend from high school days. Once there, Rachel, a communication and art major in college, landed a job as director of marketing for a retail office furniture company. She became a marathon runner and met and fell in love with Brian a geologist for the state of Arizona who was also an expedition backpacking guide at the Grand Canyon. After many, many backpacking trips together at the canyon, the question was popped and, of course, the place for the wedding was a given — the Grand Canyon. A small group of immediate family and friends gathered at a remote site at the edge of a point with a steep and deep drop off. Just before the ceremony was to begin, a Big Horn Sheep kid ascended the shear side of the cliff and joined the wedding party. He remained for the ceremony roaming between the wedding party and the guests. Just before the ceremony, Rachel presented me and her step-mom Chris with an original watercolor of the site of the wedding which she had painted in memory of her mother. The expansive vista, the wedding site, the watercolor, the happy couple, the uninvited but welcome guest — it was all awe-inspiring. I viewed it all through tears of joy. By the way and ironically, the couple had chosen "Goats Do Roam" as the brand of wine for the reception.

The SUV Danced and Pranced
(Chosen by Sandy, Chris)

The enormous SUV danced and pranced
through the shallow stream splashing
cold, clear, mountain water and moved
quickly into the shadow of a gorgeous
landscape emerging in the bright western
sky and jumping to a wheel spinning, dust
raising stop. Between luscious takes of a
glorious, plastic steering wheel and faux-wood
dash, the plush seats made of the semi-precious
hide of a poor, old, dilapidated cow sent to
the slaughter somewhere in the flat, dusty,
smelly land of West Texas gave an award
winning performance by just sitting there
looking pretty. Who would have believed that
the old cow would be so gussied up and
have a starring role in a commercial
while the SUV belched lung-choking fumes
in what otherwise had been a pristine
place?

Quiet, Peaceful

(Chosen by Jim)

Quiet, peaceful, still
Town Square, 1971,
he swaggered out of
the theatre, a twenty-six
year old, husband, dad,
university chaplain, preacher
of peace during Viet Nam,
reached into his pocket,
pulled out his hand with
index finger and thumb
cocked, pointed here
there and everywhere:
Blam, blam, blam,
"Do you feel lucky, punk?"
uttered years before he
had a "Go ahead,
make my day" kind
of a day
after watching Dirty
Harry
stare down
the bad guy.
The preacher of peace's
adrenalin was pumpin'
flowin'. He, too, was
ready to pop the bad

guys just like a few
years before, he was
Steve McQueen in
Bullitt putting his
shoulder holster over
the arm of the chair and
looking at it in a pregnant
pause as if to ask if this
is the right way, the way
he made after the unbelievable
car chase that set the standard
for all car chases to come.
Was it Bullitt's stare at his
gun that gave him pause,
or simply the still, small
voice that won out
and kept him from ever
owning a gun? And
forty-one years later
he remembers just
how he felt that evening
and he thanks God
that he never bought
that gun.

The Young Attractive, Black, Female, Law Student
(Chosen by Mary)

The young, attractive, black,
female law student, who
just happens to be
a survivor
of sexual abuse, tried to make the
case for a society where
women don't even
have to think
about having to carry a gun
in order to deter rape,
but rather to inform
and educate
the populace, and males
in particular, to respect
women. She got
several death
threats after
being interviewed on
Fox News. She
refuses to be
bullied
into silence. Good for
her, but until we attain
the status of
being an
ideal pacifistic society, I
would suggest she
carry a canister of
bear spray.

On a Sidewalk Sale Saturday
(Chosen by Marcia)

On a Sidewalk Sale Saturday
and the weather was just fine,
on a Sidewalk Sale Saturday
and I knew some great sale I'd find,
but on that sun-filled, breezy day
a little yellow piece of paper I'd find
swirling and twirling the morning away.
It caught my eye. What did I find –
a secret love note? Oh, what did it say?
I looked up and saw a wrinkled face so kind
but focused on that piece in just the same way.
A granny face, soft – she gave no mind
to anything else that day – no sway.
Her eyes followed like it was her own find,
maybe to her mind a note from a lover far away,
way back in time. Such resolve is hard to find.
And just then, the mysterious note flew away.
It just up and left without giving us any mind.
Her eyes looked into mine. She didn't look away.
Then she winked as if to say
It wasn't our day to make a great find
On a Sidewalk Sale Saturday.

Tell Me About Your Life, Dad

(Chosen by Marcia)

At sixty-seven, I still feel like a little boy when I think about my dad who died when I was seventeen.

How could I feel any differently? My life with dad never went past that.

I'm living time standing still and then in reverse. I'm getting older and he's getting younger and younger and

I'm tracing him through photos back in time to when he was a little, blond-haired, round-faced boy in scratchy, woolen

knickers standing next to his father, my grandfather,

an incredibly handsome dark-haired, dark-eyed man with a long slim face, my dad's little hand on my grandfather's forearm.

Tell me about your life, Dad, my little boy. Tell me, my poor boy, how sad it was to lose your full-bodied, big bosomed, round-faced,

beautiful, blonde mother and then that tall, dark handsome man within a few short years of each other while you were just a little boy and left all alone.

Tell me about it, Dad, and maybe, just maybe, I can help save you the terror and help you cope, cope, cope so that you wouldn't leave me alone and fatherless at seventeen.

The Blue Light in the Big Bay Window
(Chosen by Andrea)

Madison Avenue market psychologists,
like a mountain lion, a grizzly or a
Diamondback rattler knows its territory,
know what commercials to play on
just the right channels at just the right
time to generate revenues and maximize
profits for the companies that pay them,
like lobbyists in Washington DC, oh so
well. Cialis' two old-timey claw-foot tubs
appropriate for two old-timey folks are
placed between fairways and next to greens
and often close to the holes on the Golf
channel Friday, Saturday and always on
Sunday with the biggest audience as Tiger
and Phil walk past and tip their caps to the
naked bodies in the tubs and as an aside,
why are the naked bodies in separate tubs
in an ad for erectile dysfunction assuming the
dysfunction got functional? Anyway, on
the Retro channel, lawyers offer the possibility
of a big payday for sufferers of bad hip
replacements, of unmeshed uterine meshes,
for those who ingested questionable pharma-
ceuticals which may have led to cervical and
bladder cancer and mental or other physical
disabilities or who may be way in arrears on
their income taxes and insurance companies
offer million dollar term life insurance policies

for a song and banks celebrate the glories of
reverse mortgages which if left to their logical
conclusions would leave the house in the hands
of the bank at which time some other company
would offer a way out of foreclosure all seen
over and over and over night and day on the
channel where the viewers just want to watch
reruns of "The Naked City," "Route 66," and
"Mayberry R.F.D.," because they can escape
from the present and live again and again and
again in that simpler day and time all the time
in the Time Machine named Retro TV.
Is that what Madison Avenue knows in order to
help the hapless and helpless old timers looking
for a break from or maybe belated pay-dirt for all
the days' woes or is it just another target group
whose money they seek to take? At which point
Madison Avenue, Mountain Lions, Grizzlies,
Diamondback rattlers, the pharmaceutical and
insurance companies, lawyers, banks, the Naked
City detectives, and Buz and Tod and later Linc
in their Corvette, Andy, Opie and Barney whistling
on their way to the fishing hole all looked at each
other quizzically and we stared blankly at them
while Rod Serling smiled into the camera, raised
his big, black eyebrows, then frowned and announced,
"Welcome to the twilight zone" as a pedestrian
walked past the house and saw the blue light
emanating from the big, bay window just as the
police car pulled up and told the curfew violator
to get in the car.

Throwing Stones – A Short Story

(Chosen by Sandy)

One day when I was ten I went to my friend Johnny's house to play. His family lived in the house that used to be my dad's office and my Auntie Anna had lived in the back before she got so bad my dad had to take her to the Oak Lawn old peoples' home.

She was Auntie because she wasn't my dad's mom. She had been his foster mom, but her son took off for Dallas and my dad took care of her. I remember watching her give herself shots in her legs for diabetes.

At one time she had lived with us over my mother's objections, but that ended when my mother discovered that Auntie Anna used the hand towels to wipe her bottom. That was something of which my Dutch mother certainly wouldn't approve. That's when she went to live in the apartment behind my dad's office on Halsted Street before she went to Oak Lawn.

I remember going to see her in Oak Lawn. She didn't have a room. She had a bed in a long row of beds. My dad told me it was called a ward.

My dad and mom built a house on the street behind my dad's office on Halsted and my dad sold that office to Johnny's folks. They made the office into a convenience store and lived in the apartment behind it. I would go into Johnny's house and think about my Auntie Anna.

She had been a really big woman with stockings that came up to her knees. She would lift her house dress a bit to give herself the shot in the side of her thigh. I don't think she ever winced. She didn't mind spreading her legs apart and sometimes I could see the edge of her underwear. Mostly I just stood to the side and watched.

I remembered my mother saying to one of the neighbors that my Auntie Anna was no virgin when she got married and had tried it out before getting married. She said that was the way it was in Sweden. I wasn't sure what trying out marriage meant, but I couldn't imagine my Auntie Anna ever being married. She was so old and fat and had big bushy eyebrows and hair over her lip and hairy legs and she took her teeth out every night.

Johnny and I were bored that day that I went over to play and we decided to throw stones at the big, eighteen-wheel trucks that roared down Halsted. Before we knew it, a car was pulling into the parking lot in front of the store. A man got out and started yelling at us. He said we had broken his windshield.

We ran back to the house and Johnny's mom came to the side door to talk to the man. She asked us if we had been throwing stones. We said yes, but that only at the side of big trucks. We didn't think we had missed a truck and hit the windshield of the car. The man said he was going to report the incident to the police and sue us. Johnny's mom yelled at him as he walked to his car.

Later, Johnny's mom said the man couldn't be trusted because he and his kind killed Jesus.

Johnny's sister said, "Oh, mom. Jesus was a Jew."

"No he wasn't. He would never be a Jew. He was a Catholic."

Johnny's mom insisted it was true and that the killer of Jesus would say anything and they were always trying to get money and that he probably got the crack in his windshield from a stone kicked up by the tire of an eighteen-wheeler. She crossed herself.

I went home to tell my dad. I didn't think I had hit the car windshield and I didn't know if Johnny had. But I wasn't sure. I told my dad and he looked me in the eye and told me that I wasn't supposed to throw stones at trucks and we would do what was right by the man with the broken windshield.

I told my dad that I thought Jesus had died a long time ago. My dad agreed. Then I said that Johnny's mom said that the man with the broken windshield and his kind had killed Jesus.

My dad looked at me and said, "We all did, son. We all did."

Ghazal #2

(Chosen by Marilyn)

My beloved meets me halfway and teases the rest of the way
to my heart. I lace up my hiking boots and find a way

through the forest, woods, fording along the way
to the place hidden deep in the brush along the way.

Not there. Elusiveness drives me to distraction in a way
and even a compass and topographical map don't reveal a way

to your heart. So I have decided late in the day just to stay,
come what may, in one place and wait for love to come my way.

But the sky turns dark, the clouds stay with rain coming this day,
And I, the fair weather lover, will pursue my love in another way.

He Entered the Sacred Ground
(Chosen by Marilyn)

He entered the sacred ground
Through the weather-beaten arch
And wandered among the graves
With native trinkets of plastic and
Tobacco at the feet of the chipped
Paint crosses.

He walked back through the arch
To the back of the pick up truck
With the tailgate transformed into
A communion table. He got into
Line and soon consumed the broken
Body and spilled blood of Jesus

In a Graham cracker and orange juice.
He walked over to the edge and stood
In the shadow of death in the valley of
Wounded Knee. He stood perfectly
Still and completely quiet and heard
The heart piercing cries

And screams like arrows shot out of
The mouths of old men, women and
Children. The summer sun beat down
On his head, but he felt the winter wind
Whip the snow around his feet. He saw the
Rifle placed in the dead

Old man's frozen hand and he wept.

Fire Consumes Wood

(Chosen by Matthew)

His eyes caught the line,
"Fire consumes wood...
as time consumes us," and
he lingered awhile. He set
the novel aside, glanced at the
candles burning in the fireplace
and looked at his legs crossed
on the ottoman like two dogs
from the same litter resting
heads crossed at the
crook of their necks. The
dogs lifted their heads and
rubbed each other's noses
and then lay still. He saw the
spider veins crawling around
the sides of his ankles, the
scar on the shin from when
a board dropped and cleanly
sliced the skin to the bone
forty some years ago as he
helped clean up a house after
a tornado ripped through his
Old Kentucky Hometown. He
rubbed the faint scar on his knee
which once was a gaping wound
and recalled the fall from the
tree in his eighth grade girl

friend's backyard as he was
trying to show off and how
the bark just like number
ten sandpaper instantaneously
left the sheath over the knee cap
exposed for all the world, not
to mention his then former
girlfriend, to see. He winced
recalling the alcohol being
poured copiously into the wound
by his mother and how she furiously
scrubbed out the dirt and
meticulously tweezed the slivers
from the flesh as if she were
plucking her eyebrows on a
Sunday morning before church.
He picked gently at a scab on his
other knee from a scrape on the
rough wall of the pool just days
before. He tightened his thigh
muscles and recalled significant
definition from years of cycling
and jogging where now wrinkles
looked up and smiled deviously.
He rubbed his legs, slapped his
thighs and said, "Time to get up,
boys. I need another cup of coffee."

A Quarter Mile Down the Gravel Road
(Chosen by Matthew)

A quarter-mile down the gravel road, he saw the four there
And when he drove in the drive he felt a cold, icy stare,
From the son and daughter who made for the front door.
He then caught a view of the man named Joe on the riding mower.

He was here to see Joe and the family in such great need.
He climbed out of the car; Joe's wife moved to intercede.
The mower had stopped, all things still and cold and distant,
She stopped him like a yellow police barrier insistent

That he watch out for her beloved who cut paths on the mower
Else she and her man and woman child would show him the door.
He meant no harm, but they were understandably protective
Of the man who was husband and dad and unprotected

Now with a disabling disease, something that made ill at ease
Everyone in the family and his guess everyone who tried to please
Those who were going through anticipatory grief and disbelief
Like the wife and son and daughter who stand in bass relief

On the grounds of the house that has the imprint of the man
All over it, house and yard and poll barn and vegetable garden.
The man named Joe, still big and strong and looking powerful
Had stopped the mower and everything became peaceful.

He had pulled, laboriously, one hand from the steering wheel
The key being turned with fingers that still had some feel,
Offering up that big, banana fingered hand with insistence
The other forearm, lifting and holding with patient persistence.

It was as if he was struggling to be as gracious as possible
Under the circumstances when the host should be hospitable,
But that was the way it was the visitor would find out
Over the course of months and months of family being stout

And Joe being gracious, hospitable and one of a kind
It seemed to the one who visited over and over in his mind.
Time went by and weekly visits progressed with mother
Son and daughter spirited away in the kitchen with another

Friend of the family. They still seemed suspicious of him
Who had driven up the drive that fall day and had seen them
In all their vulnerability, unable to change reality and no power
To make Lou Gehrig go away, that shadow who would glower

Over the ever weakening body of the man of the house
And make everyone there feel as if they had a dose
Of cold water tossed in their face. Wake up, wake up to reality!
No, no! Each would shout from the kitchen into eternity.

Joe's voice was soft and warm like a late spring rain
He comforted the visitor with the ever same refrain

Which must have driven the family to distraction from the other
room as they heard him speak of prayer and the loving cover

Of God over all of them. They felt only cold, piercing ice
Falling from the gutterless roof on their heads making a slice
Neat and quick which cut them to the quick, the shaft securing
Them to the ground, they were unable to move, no turning

Around, standing frozen by the kitchen sink hating more and more
The sounds of sadness spoken ever more quietly and uttered for
Peace and serenity. Joe couldn't move his now thin, limp body
And his voice was so quiet even the attentive ears heard nobody.

The visitor knelt close to Joe's supine stance to hear
And feel the soft, warm loving breath on his cheek, a whisper.
Joe saw the visitor's tears stream down his face and he saw
The shoulders shaking, so with enormous will, Joe lifted his paw-

Like hand raised up with the monumental persistence
The visitor had seen in the fall. Now, done again with insistence
And placed, not dropped, on the folded hands of the weeping
Visitor. It was Joe's benediction for the visitor's keeping.

They just stayed in that place of grace and the visitor could
See Lou standing with hat over heart while thousands stood
To hear him speak through tears the words unfurled
That he was the luckiest man in the world.

Joe's eyes were shut, his breathing shallow
The family stood at the door sensing they needed to follow
Through the thin place into that sacred space
Of peace, and love and Eternal Grace.

The Proverb Admonishes
(Chosen by Chris)

The proverb admonishes, "Don't
    get between a she-bear and her
cubs." They sat and watched
    the survival of the fittest being
played out at what otherwise
    would have been the terrifying
distance of twelve feet, but
    even the adventurous camera-
man wisely used his high
    powered zoom lens as mother
bison tried to protect their
    young from mother wolves
who desperately needed to
    feed their pups back in the
winter's den. A bison calf
    lay mauled but not killed
by a mother wolf who sat
    staring from a safe distance
of perhaps twelve feet.
    The calf's mother licked the
wounds and snorted and shook
    her head defiantly at the wolf.
Both mothers left at night fall
    to return at daybreak where
they found the calf who had
    survived the cold, lonely,
painful night, futilely strugg-
    ling to stand at its mother's
urging to flee for the safety
    of the woods. She licked and

nudged in patient desperation
     while the mother wolf sat near-
by. The mother bison watched
     her calf struggle and fall. She
then turned and left her still
     breathing calf to catch the herd.
The mother wolf moved in
     for the kill. Her pups would
survive and grow, play and
     frolic in the verdant spring
fields until the day a big, male
     black bear visited. For how long
did the mother bison miss, ache
     and long for the calf she had to
abandon? For the moment, the
     two viewers felt the conflict of
joy and sorrow from the safe
     distance of twelve feet.

In the Warmth of Winter
(Chosen by Matthew, Andrea)

It was cold and clear the night we walked down the rural Kentucky road. We had parked the cars in the gravel driveway of one home, and after squeezing thirteen teenage and four adult bodies into the small, enclosed porch and singing three familiar carols, we were walking toward another home nearby.

The stars were all over the sky, but the moon must have headed south for the winter. The faint light emanating from the stars wasn't enough to illuminate the road ahead, so we groped along by memory and by the sound of our shoes striking the recently laid macadam.

The young people weren't as cautious as we adults were, and I worried that one or two of the more rambunctious youths would twist an ankle running off and on the road or would dart into an unseen barbed wire fence and tear a new winter coat or, what's worse, some tender adolescent skin.

I also kept my ear attuned to the sounds around us in the hope that the shrill bark of a farm dog would not pierce through the sounds of the incessant giggling and periodic shouts of trumped-up, young, male bravado. After riding my bike over country roads and being chased seemingly for miles by huge, farm mongrels, I had developed not only respect for but a dreadful fear of those dogs.

Walking behind the teenage voices, which served as a directional guide, I ventured a prolonged gaze at the moonless, December sky. It was kaleidoscopic. As I turned my head, the black and white patterns seemed to change. I was taken back in time to the warm summer nights when, as a teenager myself, I worked as a church camp lifeguard and recreation director.

After all the campers and counselors had gone to their cabins and were asleep, I would leave my trailer, walk up a treeless hill next to the camp custodian's house, lie back in his chaise lounge and stare into the heavens. The winter sky was as magnificent as I remember that summer sky to be.

A number of years had passed since that camp experience, and I wondered why I had never really taken the time to explore and study the astronomical sights above me. How little I knew of God's universe.

The porch light directly ahead signaled the next stop on our winter's pilgrimage. As we all gathered at the side door of that small, old farmhouse and began to sing, "Hark, the Herald Angels Sing," an elderly couple came to the door and stepped coatless into the cold night.

I wiggled my now numb toes trying to get some circulation going, pulled back the top of each glove and blew my moist, warm breath over the palms of my hands down to the freezing fingertips. The old couple wasn't even shivering. He put his arm around her delicate but stooped shoulders and she snuggled against his once strong but now aged chest. Their eyes were rimmed with water and as a tear fell upon her cheek, I wondered if it would feel cold on her face as the night air blew against it.

We stood there no more than a few minutes. When the songs were over, the carolers waved, shouted "Merry Christmas" and, now that they were more familiar with the contour of the land, began to run back to the cars. I walked up to the couple and, in silence, shook his large and still calloused hand and then leaned over and pressed my lips to her soft, tear-moistened cheek.

As I walked back to the cars with the other chaperones, I felt very good and very warm.

He Exited This Life

(Chosen by Sandy, Mary)

He exited this life
near the end of
his sixth decade.

He thought the door
locked at the
attempts made

to shake the open
door, push and pull
with energy to fade

away from trying
any longer than he
could have stayed

and so he did
what everyone on
earth forbade.

He sat beside himself
without meds that
might have saved

him to think, but he
still couldn't get in
so he made

the decision to leave
abruptly and adieu
he bade.
That's the unnecessary and
tragic thing he
decided to do

and left so many to wonder
for years how to bid him
a very good adieu.

He Impatiently Awaited His Leash

(Chosen by Rachel, Mary)

He impatiently awaited his leash.
He hurriedly tugged at his collar.
He loudly barked disturbing the peace.
He stopped in his tracks when he heard the holler,
That came resoundingly from his master's mouth,
That fell on the ears of all who were near,
And he felt the yank and tug that left no doubt
That he needed to stand still in a little fear
Of displeasing the one who had come to mean so much,
The one who loved him through and through
And the superlative other who made such a fuss and such
Over a love of the dog who proved so true,
Over the very dog who proved so true,
The now late chocolate lab who proved so very, very true
The one who has left the man and the his wife
The dog's alpha and omega,
The truly sad two,
Alone and knowing that he was
The alpha and omega of dogs
For those two, now so alone as they look at the couch
And the chair where he slept and the box of his
Toys, yes, those, so lonely in the box, too.

Sometimes He Would Call
(In memory of Lon.)

Sometimes, when he thought too much time had passed without a poem appearing, he would call and ask, "Are you all right?"

I would chuckle, tell him I was fine, thank him for his concern and tell him a poem would appear soon. It was a catalyst.

The Big Bay Window
(Chosen by Marcia, Sandy, Rachel)

He kept waiting for his dad to come home,
to walk down the street, 144th Street to be exact.
Actually, his dad had never done that before
to the best of his memory. His dad drove just
about every where, but for some reason the
seventeen-year-old, senior in high school,
stood in the living room staring blankly out the
big bay window expecting, hoping, desiring, crying
out in a stone, cold, silent way to see his dad,
his dad walking home. His dad didn't do that,
nor did his dad do it when the son slept dreaming
that his dad would walk down 144th street on the
man's way home. His dad didn't walk down the
street and he didn't come home, the dad's home,
the son's home, their home. His dad wouldn't
ever again sit in the chair by that big, bay window
smoking his Chesterfield non-filter cigarettes pulling
deeply on a draw and exhaling with utter satisfaction
while he told his son never ever to start the filthy habit.
His dad would never again lie down on the couch
under the big, bay window with pains shooting
down his arms, saying to his son when he walked in
the room after school one day that he needed to be driven
ASAP to the hospital because his dad really wasn't
feeling very well at all and the boy knew that it must be

pretty serious. His dad came home from the hospital two
weeks later in a really weakened state after the son
had visited him only twice during that time because
it was the boy's senior year and he was really busy
with which whatever it is that seniors in high school
are busy, not to mention never ending a sentence
with a dangling participle no matter how awkward
it makes the sentence his teachers had always told
him. His father lived another year but didn't work
much and every penny that his father made from his
work came in to keep things going and if he didn't
work, it didn't come in and it weighed heavily on his
dad's mind, ever so heavily and the boy knew it. So
one evening when his dad was feeling up to it, he
left the house to make house calls to sell head stones
to those who had recently lost loved ones or to put it
more bluntly, who had loved ones die. The son was
napping on the couch and his father's words as
he walked out the door were that the boy shouldn't
sleep the evening away and that he should get up and
do his homework. Next thing the boy knew the phone
was ringing and it was a call from the police station that
his dad had stepped in front of a train and had been killed.
The son thought the officer actually said that his dad had killed
himself. The boy said it was a joke. The police officer officiously
said no. The boy called his married sister and they picked up
their mom from her work as a sales person in a women's dress

shop. They went to view the body, that is, his brother-in-law, his
sister's husband actually viewed the remains and said he
would never, ever speak of it again. And so, for a long time
the son stood looking out of that big, bay window for his
dad to walk down 144th Street, and then after the house
was sold and he and his mom moved and then moved
and moved again, of course, the son couldn't look out
the big, bay window waiting for his dad to come home,
but he couldn't stop dreaming that he was standing in
front of that window watching and waiting for his dad
to come home. Through college, graduate school,
marriage, birth of his son and daughter and moving
to another state, and then one day he realized
that he didn't dream that dream any more and that
he just remembered being a seventeen-year-old waiting
for his dad to come home. Then one day I got a call and
knew I would never get another call of his concern for me.
He had died, tragically, violently in a moment of utter,
personal despair. I haven't written much since he died
and it occurred to me that if it were any other time,
I might expect a phone call of his concern for me,
a call which he won't be making ever again, but just
the thought of his calling was enough for me to write this.

He Wondered Where and When

He wondered where
the cheerleaders were.
He didn't expect to hear
them chant and watch
them leap and jump
and form a perky pyra-
mid immediately after
he bowed out, gave
his final farewell –
a bit like Lou Gehrig
addressing the throngs
who gathered on July
4th 1939 in the Bronx's
Holy of Holies, a place
where bombs went off
regularly in celebration,
but only to a small con-
gregation he had known
for a mere twenty months.
But a few years later, he
did think it would be nice
if someone pierced the
silence and said he was the
best – preacher, pastor, ad-
ministrator (a poet, a proph-
et, a priest and a king), but
he sits in silence and listens
to the roar of appreciation
or is that just the pesky ring-
ing in his ears at 6:54 a.m

on July 4th as he sips his
French Press coffee now
that the Krups thirty-year-old
coffee maker the kids had
given his late wife had given
up the ghost just the day be-
fore? And so, he has himself
and, of course, the letters of
one Saul of Tarsus known,
post conversion, as Paul the
Apostle who called himself
the Least of All Apostles in
a tone filled with what sounds
like false modesty and who
probably would have loved
being addressed as Saint
Paul if he had lived long
enough to hear the acco-
lades which were still centur-
ies on down the line. Perhaps
as a way of coping with the
fact that Caesar was about
to put an end to his earthly
existence wrote, "I have fought
the good fight; I have finished
the race…" and in the spirit
of delayed gratification
concluded the thought with,
"…henceforth, there is a
crown…for me…" to be

placed upon his head sometime in the future on the Day when the bombs of joy get belted out of the park like Yankee Stadium in about 1934. He would take comfort in Paul's postponement if he believed in return appearances by popular demand but he had only been asked back to a congregation once in forty-three years. So, for now people crawl out of bed, shower, eat breakfast and go to work without ever giving him so much as a passing thought if for no other reason than they don't know him from Adam and those who do have moved on with life in most respects except for those caught in a time warp of hoping hopelessly for the Cubs who continue to toil in the friendly confines of Wrigley Field where hardly is heard the clear crack of the Louisville Slugger on a ball for a Texas Leaguer let alone a home run.

Black Friday from the Edge of the Sea

We are awash in a sea
of horrendous violence
on the mean streets
of America and often
in the elementary, high
schools, colleges and
universities, but
still…
hip, politically progressive
Hollywood churns out
mayhem as entertain-
ment with celebrities
brandishing assault
rifles, hand guns and
grenades
in the hands of those
who speak out and
march for gun
control
when the imaginary shoot-
ing on set ends. We're
drowning
while…
hypocritical Hollywood
flaps its water wings
in the shallow end
of the
pool.

Carpentry and Gardening

My wife's mixed media sculptures are a lot like carpentry.
Once the fabric is cut and the wood is sawed and the clay
is molded and the rest is glued it is pretty well history.
My poetry is much like gardening — moving words, phrases,
line lengths, endings, beginnings, working the soil
of the poem's bloom.
The pressure is on; she has to get it just right
and I just have to till the soil
sometimes at midnight
under a full moon.

Some People Are Beaten Down So Hard

Some people are beaten down so hard
by life and then there are those who
are beaten down for their sake. He thinks
of when he was a young boy in his grandmother's
kitchen watching her pound the
big mound of dough into submission with
her wood pastry roller and then sprinkling
the carcass with white embalming dust and
rolling out the body with the rolling-pin — back
and forth, back and forth — until it was as flat as
she wanted it to be, except the dough didn't
bleed, never bled like those always do who stand
up to oppression and suffer the batons of bigotry.
They bleed and some die as the injustice rolls
over them like his grandmother's roller, but as
with his grandmother's dough, when she put it in
the oven, it wasn't to burn it to ashes but to watch
it warm and rise and form a beautiful crust to
protect that which was so light and tender inside.
The protesters don't rise like a Phoenix from the
ashes, rather they rise in resurrection and their
blood forms a beautiful, brown crust to be broken
at the dinner table while Jesus' followers consume
the delicious, divine, life-giving bread.

Ecological Racism and Karma

Why do we always see
minorities suffering when we
view environmental
disasters on our
T.V.'s from our living
rooms? Because the
minorities have always
been relegated to those
vulnerable and unwanted
areas like Indians
relegated to barren
reservations?
Will it always be
that way or, perhaps,
through the egalitarianism
of global warming, the blacks
and browns and maybe even
the reds at the Four Corners
and Wounded Knee know
something about karma
and the future of places
like Naples, Florida when
you see them
smile?

Some NSA Guy

Some NSA guy sat in an office somewhere in obscurity, not unlike a drone pilot on the third floor of an office building in downtown Wichita or wherever. The NSA guy, fortunately not the drone pilot, sat staring at us through our T.V. Our Chocolate Lab wasn't feeling well and laid at my wife's feet under a blanket. We hoped he didn't have Valley Fever, a fungal disease which gets in the lungs and not excitement over ASU's sports teams. We wondered if the NSA guy felt sorry for Buddy Baloo and offered a prayer for him from his office in obscurity. The show we were watching was a bit boring so to entertain ourselves we waved at the NSA guy. To spice things up for the guy during this festive holiday season, I asked my wife to remove her shirt and bra. Chagrined, she just stared at me and turned and stuck her tongue out at the NSA guy I guess for invading our privacy without asking permission. I hope she won't be carted off to Guantanamo but perhaps she will have already been released during Obama's first term because that is what he promised, so she would be back home with her feet up on the ottoman like now. But it is well into his second term, so I guess, if she does go, she won't be getting out any time soon unless Congress decides to get a life and stops trying to sabotage the president and actually votes to shut the thing down. I'm sure it would make Fidel and his brother Raul happy not to mention my wife and the dog who misses her already and that's probably why he isn't feeling very well, so it's a relief to know that he doesn't have Valley Fever after all. Meanwhile, my wife's feet are still on the ottoman and the NSA guy is counting each toe, but the drone pilot apparently doesn't know, thank the Lord.

The Cowboy from Tucson

"Old cowboys don't pass on.
They just spend the day
in the barn napping on the hay
with all their cowboy duds
still on."

There was an old man from Tucson
who slept with his boots and spurs on.
His wife told him to go find some old mare
and with that gave him a real mean stare.
So, he then slept in the barn on the hay
with his boots and spurs still on.

There was an old man from Tucson
who slept with his six-shooter on.
It went off by accident one night
and gave his wife a mighty fright.
He then slept in the barn on the hay
with his six-shooter still on.

There was an old man from Tucson
who slept with his old chaps on.
He mounted his wife and rubbed her legs raw,
so he then slept in the barn on the straw

but, by God, he had his boots, spurs,
six-shooter and chaps still on.

The Religious Rich

The religious rich, coldly, savagely,
with the wicked wonder of sub-
stitutionary atonement as their
rationale, look upon all those below
them economically, morally,
religiously as, inherently, unworthy.
It's a moral issue, naturally, they say.
Freedom requires hard work and that
is missing, of course, and we have
given more than enough time, they say.
The rich may not have gotten to where
they are in the God forsaken hierarchy
through any effort of their own as second
or third generationalists, rather perhaps
through the avaricious grasping of their
parents, grandparents and on and on,
but however they got it, it is a provid-
ential gift that gives them the right to
call all those below, and that means a
heck of a lot, to shape up, measure up
or give it up and get lost and better than
that, just plain vanish, please, they ask,
demand and pour a pittance of their
riches into keeping those who are not

like them, if only on surface appearances as brown or black or gay, because they pollute life, down and out. And so, democracy is gone, brought to the curb and tossed under the bus by avaricious capitalism crouched in escatalogical terms of hyper-evangelical Christianity fighting for Jerusalem and hurrying the second return, a pause to meet Jesus in the sky and then the blessed, justifying, satisfying, blood slaking Armageddon when God finally will obliterate the unworthy (of course, we all are unworthy they would demure but then we are the elect they would declare) and the one percent of one percent will meet and greet the greatest defender of conservative moralist causes, the righteously and justly avaricious capitalist of all eternity – Jesus, the Capitalistic Christ, who will establish the Dow Jones and the S and P on the Dome of the Rock for ever and ever, amen and amen.

The String of Jalapeno Lights

He hung the string of jalapeño shaped festive lights
from the Arizona condo balcony heights,

and saw at the swimming pool beneath
a shapely young lady in a swim suit so brief.

He leaned too far over to see down the suit top
and did his best holiday salsa belly-flop.

The young lady heard the big plop and knelt
over the poor rube,

who, now unconscious, couldn't appreciate her,
ah, cleavage

Way Out in the Wild and Wooly West

Way out in the wild and wooly West,
they found a downtown Phoenix deli
with online reviews proclaiming it the best,
for specialty goodies like Swedish fish so smelly.

Till Christmas they put off the Lutefisk and headcheese
but saw windmill blades blowing a zephyr breeze.
Yes, they found a box of cookies baked by the Dutch.
They paid and said, "Thank you so much,"

and tack sa mycket in Swedish and eet smakelijk (bon appetite) in Dutch.

In the car, the passenger so eager, tore the box with her bare hands,
and they both partook of the contents made in Ooltgensplaat, the Netherlands.

The driver was of Swedish and Dutch tribes
and his wife of German and Irish descent
but both agreed it was a few U.S. dollars
very well spent

When Was the Last Time

When was the last time,
you hugged your brother,
you American Capitalistic,
blue-collar or merchant class,
maybe middle-class
Christian you, your brother –
you know the one who
stands in line to get a job,
any job for that matter, or
his sister, your sister,
who stands in line next to
your brother in that same rain
for hours – the two of them
who when they come out
of the rain when their number
is up, and that number is called
with a certain disdain
have to face some faceless,
officious, condescending
bureaucrat who hopes eternally,
because he or she sits
in a dry place in a gray,

aluminum, glass, dry-walled,
soulless room and hasn't
stood outside in the
cold, November rain that he or
she might, by the grace of the
good, white people's God,
spend some federally
mandated Christmas break-time
with the senators, representatives,
lobbyists and the billionaires
behind them all at a $500 a
plate holiday fund-raiser
for people who despise people
like your brother, your sister,
the officious bureaucrat
and you, too, old man?

Art Acknowledgements

The artwork, illustrations, hand-lettering and photos were added to run parallel to the stories. The goal was not to distract you from the words but simply to enhance your experience. I hope you enjoyed the journey.

I would like to acknowledge the following contributors. All other drawings, paintings and hand-lettering illustrations are done by myself.

- Rachel Dahl

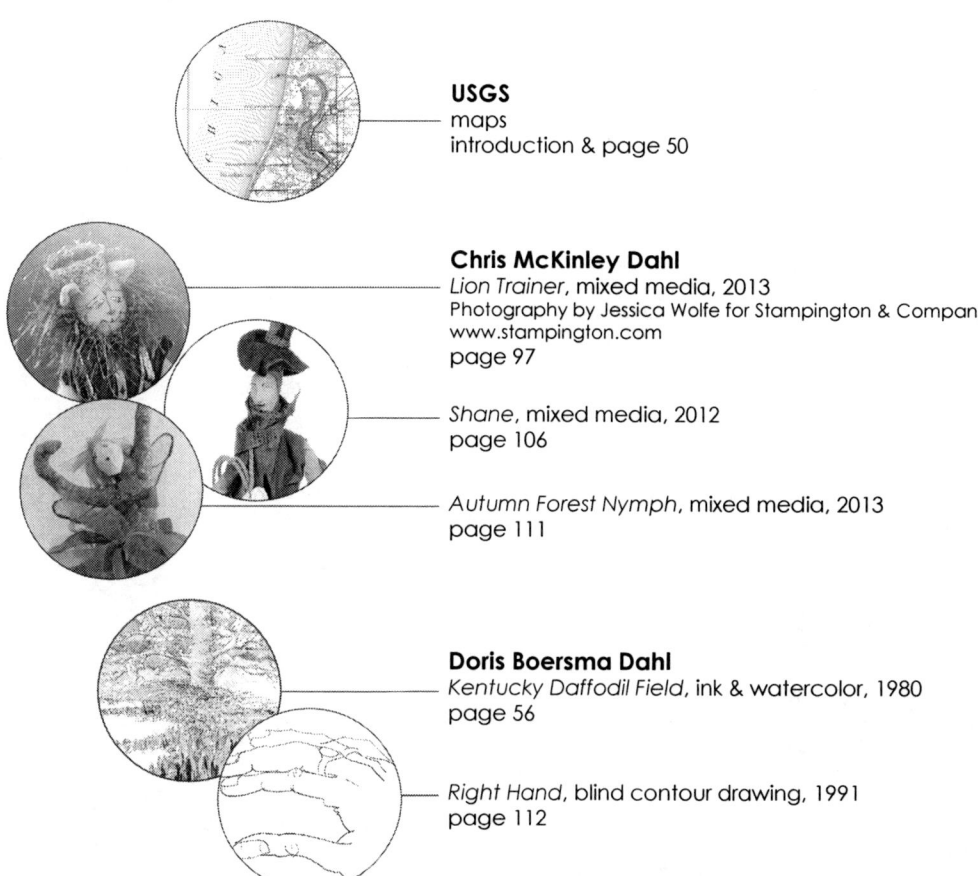

USGS
maps
introduction & page 50

Chris McKinley Dahl
Lion Trainer, mixed media, 2013
Photography by Jessica Wolfe for Stampington & Company
www.stampington.com
page 97

Shane, mixed media, 2012
page 106

Autumn Forest Nymph, mixed media, 2013
page 111

Doris Boersma Dahl
Kentucky Daffodil Field, ink & watercolor, 1980
page 56

Right Hand, blind contour drawing, 1991
page 112

CPSIA information can be obtained
at www.ICGtesting.com
Printed in the USA
FFOW02n1828050814
6717FF

9 780990 426318